The Opiate

Books

Published by The Opiate Books 2021, 1ˢᵗ update 2022.

Copyright of *Yet So As By Fire* belongs to Anton Bonnici

Cover design by Jac Capra

Cover image by Luana Montebello; @introverted_bookworm

Performance rights for this work are held by Anton Bonnici. For more information, please get in touch via thisisnottheatre.com

This play is dedicated to my father, Joseph Bonnici (1955-2002).

Among other things a teacher, poet and writer, my father's death certificate will forever note *"death by natural causes"*.

This play will serve as a reminder that, for all intents and purposes, he was ultimately killed by the Maltese political class.

# Yet So As By Fire

A Passion Play in Two Acts
by Anton Bonnici

Foreword
by Genna Rivieccio

# Contents

# Foreword

Until encountering Anton, my familiarity with Malta was, at best, limited to the bizarre early 00s era in pop culture history where every movie of an "epic" genre seemed to mention filming there (perhaps proving that the island is nothing more than a tax haven). This included *Troy* and *Gladiator*. Hence, photo reports of Orlando Bloom and Brad Pitt being spotted there while on set, complete with candids published in gossip rags like *Us Weekly* splashed alongside pictures of Britney Spears (the closest thing to Maltese royalty there is in the U.S.). Later on, there was another Pitt movie, *World War Z*, which Anton himself actually appeared in as an extra (of course, he wouldn't want that mentioned, as it could end up turning into this out-of-control sort of lore, like *Once Upon a Time in Hollywood*'s Rick Dalton constantly having to talk about how he was *almost* [but not really] chosen as the lead in *The Great Escape* instead of Steve McQueen).

Before this 00s period during which a burst of Hollywood activity put a spotlight on the island to someone as middle-class as myself, maybe *The Maltese Falcon* was all I really knew of Malta, a film that doesn't really utilize the island at all. What I'm getting at is, Malta is largely shrouded in mystery to anyone living outside of Europe (and even to those living in Europe), especially Americans. Any American who tells you differently is either bluffing or Pete Buttigieg. The point is, this world is overdue for a veracious portrait of the island, from someone who was actually born and raised there. What's more, someone who is, to put it frankly, "no bullshit." So yes, this automatically excludes Christopher Marlowe.

With Anton's passion play, *Yet So As By Fire*, those who exist outside the island are at last given that long-overdue portrait. One that does away with vague depictions primarily highlighting a picturesque and idyllic vacation spot for the rich to stop by in their yacht on the way to the Greek islands. One that accents the hypocrisy of religion and how the devil can always cite Scripture for his purpose.

To emphasize this notion, we have at the center of the play Victoria Sultana, a hyper-pious woman who runs a pair of religious magazines and shows early signs of bearing the wounds of stigmata. In the wake of her death, she is elevated to the level of a saint, whereas in life she was viewed as a rather irritating presence. Ain't that always the way? But what Anton establishes from the outset in his very first scene description is that beneath the "rustic" and "unspoiled" charm of Malta is corruption, greed and competition to the literal death.

We are all born to our unavoidable fate. Some portents of that fate indicate it's going to be a rougher road than it might be for others. In Anton's case, perhaps being born in a small town called Pietà was one indication of the path ahead. But here, within the damning lines of this much-needed play, Anton will show no mercy to the island that shaped him. He will only show how it ends up shaping others who stay.

Genna Rivieccio

Editor-in-Chief, *The Opiate*

Editor, The Opiate Books

# Play Notes

The events of this play take place on the island of Malta in 2010, a year before the referendum that would legalize divorce. This is a work of fiction. All characters and events are fictional and any resemblance to real life people or situations is purely coincidental.

**Characters:**

TV Journalist – A person in their thirties.

Victoria Sultana – A woman in her forties.

George Sultana / Husband – A man in his forties. Husband to Victoria Sultana.

Pierre Buhagiar / Brother – A man in his early forties. Brother to Victoria Sultana.

Filomena Buhagiar / Mother – A woman in her early sixties. Mother to Victoria Sultana.

First Lady – A woman in her early sixties. Wife of the President of Malta.

Magistrate – A man in his early sixties.

Family Doctor – A man in his late sixties.

Victoria's Secretary – A woman in her late thirties.

Intern – A woman in her early twenties.

Secretary of the Curia / Priest – A priest in his fifties.

Exorcist – A priest in his fifties.

Psychologist – A person in their thirties.

Mariella Spiteri / Blogger – A woman in her thirties.

**Set:**     The set is a house with two floors connected via staircase, and a back garden. This takes up all upstage space, spreading onto centre stage and downstage right. Upstairs we see a bedroom and downstairs we see a kitchen leading onto a garden further down stage. For Act One, this is Victoria's and George's residence, with a middle-class tone and a clean domestic appeal, including a small TV screen in the kitchen. At the corner, downstage right of the garden, is a statue of Mother Mary.

For Act Two, the set becomes the Sultana family home. Same upstairs/downstairs structure but is decorated to look older, a more luxurious and stately residence. On this set the garden is clearly set for a party and, instead of the statue, there is an easel upon which a scene-specific painting shall be placed. Downstage left has a more flexible open space for both acts where scenes that are not situated inside the residences can take place.

**TV Show:** The public TV Friday night talk show *THE TALK* scenes of the play are to be pre-filmed and projected somewhere off stage without interfering with the performance of Victoria's story. It is very important that the actors playing the family members being interviewed on TV are different from the actors playing the same characters onstage, though there should be some resemblance. The implication needs to be that the ones in the filmed TV interviews are the 'real' people, whereas onstage, performers are portraying them. This effect could also be achieved using makeup.

**N.B.:** / means the next line overlaps here.

# Act One

00

## ONSCREEN

*The island of Malta. Blue sea. Quaint towns. Historic sights and churches. Lots of churches. Church bells can be heard ringing. The projection starts off on a stereotypical, touristy visual presentation of the island but escalates into an unbearable cacophony of church bells, with a bombardment of churches, hotels, and construction sites.*

## CUT TO JOURNALIST

01

## ONSCREEN – THE TALK

JOURNALIST:  Good evening, ladies and gentlemen. Welcome to yet another episode of The Talk. A few weeks ago, our country lost one of its brightest, holiest stars. Victoria Sultana died on Friday the 23rd of May to the shock and astonishment of all. In today's program we will be looking at the life of Victoria Sultana, including her final hours, as we attempt to understand better her great mystery. Here, in the company of her family and friends, filmed for the occasion of tonight's program, we have some sincere answers to the only question we are all asking, should Victoria Sultana be declared a saint?

CUT TO FIRST LADY

*The First Lady appears onscreen, sitting on a high armchair, with a caption underneath giving us her name and a short description of her relation to Victoria. The description says, 'mentor and best friend'.*

FIRST LADY:   I believe Victoria Sultana is a saint whether she is officially declared so or not. I have known this for as long as I have known Victoria. By her example, by her devotion, by her sacrifice and grace, mind, body and soul, Victoria Sultana has always been a saint walking amongst us. It is our turn now to devote our life to her like she devoted hers to us, I will advocate for her sainthood until I give up my own ghost.

CUT TO BROTHER

*Dr Pierre Buhagiar, "Member of the European Parliament, son of the late Prime Minister Emeritus Godwin Buhagiar, brother of the late Victoria M. Sultana"*

BROTHER:     Whether my sister Victoria Sultana is declared a saint or not should remain within the jurisdiction of those who are in authority to ultimately make such decisions. But I will always believe in Victoria, I will always believe in my sister. My sister has always been a holy woman, graced by the immediate presence of our Lord in her life. Victoria did not merely have faith, Victoria lived her faith, her faith was her life. This is the woman I had the God-given fortune to grow and live with under the same roof of our happy home as brother and sister, and with her in my life, I'm not ashamed to say that I myself have been graced with her spiritual devotion since my earliest memories.

CUT TO JOURNALIST & HUSBAND

JOURNALIST:     Mr Sultana, do you believe your late wife, Victoria Sultana, should be declared a saint?

*Mr George Sultana "Chief advisor to the Minister of Finance and husband of the late Victoria M. Sultana"*

HUSBAND:    She was my wife, and I loved her as a wife. I was married to Victoria for twenty-four years. She was, and in my eyes will forever remain, the perfect wife any God-fearing husband could wish for, and I will be forever grateful to have been blessed with such a marriage. Should my wife be declared a saint? I don't know. But was I married to a saint? Yes, I believe so.

FADE TO BLACK

02

ONSTAGE

*For all of ACT 1 the set is decorated to represent VICTORIA's house. Light on the upstairs bedroom. HUSBAND & VICTORIA are in bed. VICTORIA rises out of the bed, rather stiffly, she cranes her neck stretching it.*

VICTORIA:    The Lord is my light and my salvation; whom shall I fear?

*We can see that she is wearing gloves as with a gloved hand she switches off the alarm. Then she picks up a wooden crucifix from her bedside table. It's big enough to be held in both hands. And she lowers herself to the floor beside her bed, kneeling as she puts the crucifix to her forehead.*

VICTORIA:     Dear God, please bless me with your divine help to live once again a whole new day in your service. Protect me from the temptations of the proud pagans and empower me against the corruption of the minions of Satan. Please oh Lord, let me be an ever-truthful witness to your Word, your Son, Jesus Christ our Saviour, Amen.

*After which VICTORIA pulls the crucifix from her forehead, brings it to her mouth in an intense devotion and kisses the figure of the Christ with slightly open, trembling lips.*

BLACKOUT

03

*Now VICTORIA is in the kitchen making coffee. HUSBAND has woken up and is dressed for work. He opens a drawer in the bedroom and chooses a tie. He puts the tie around his neck and is about to start coming down the stairs when he pauses and walks back to the bedroom. VICTORIA looks up from downstairs as if sensing her husband's unusual hesitation. She looks at her watch and looks back up. HUSBAND knots his own tie diligently upstairs and adjusts it until it's in place. He goes back to the drawer, takes out a small bottle of cologne and puts a drop on his neck before putting the bottle back. By now VICTORIA has walked to the bottom of the stairs and is waiting for him. He sees her midway down and they both pause. VICTORIA on the first step downstairs, HUSBAND a couple of steps down from upstairs. HUSBAND looks impeccable; he continues descending the stairs confidently, with an air of near superiority. VICTORIA is taken aback with his demeanour.*

HUSBAND:     Good morning.

VICTORIA:     Good morning to you too. Is everything okay?

HUSBAND:     Of course, why wouldn't it be?

VICTORIA:     I don't know, you came down a bit later than usual, I thought maybe you're not feeling well.

HUSBAND:     I'm fine.

*He kisses her on the forehead from a step above hers. She is shocked by the gesture and takes a step back.*

HUSBAND:     It's only a kiss dear.

VICTORIA:     It's not that. (*She gets closer and smells him.*) What's this cologne you're wearing?

HUSBAND:     Oh that, it's just a little something I picked up after work, fancied something different. Why, you don't like it?

VICTORIA:     There's nothing wrong with it, I guess I just wasn't expecting it that's all.

HUSBAND:     Listen, I was thinking, why don't we go on a little holiday? Pack a little suitcase each and disappear for a couple of days?

VICTORIA:     George, you know that's impossible.

HUSBAND:     Why? Why is it impossible?

VICTORIA:     Because I have a million important things to do which I can't just drop to have a holiday, that's why. What's gotten into you?

HUSBAND:     You are right of course, you are right. It's just a small whim I woke up with that's all. (*continues walking down the stairs and past VICTORIA heading for the kitchen*) You'll do fine Victoria, I know you will. Everything will be fine.

VICTORIA:     What do you mean I'll "do fine"?

HUSBAND:     I mean with work and, you know, your mission and your plans; I know you won't give up.

VICTORIA:     You know I love my work; why should I give up? I have God by my side; of course I'll be fine. You're behaving terribly strange this morning George. Are you sure nothing is the matter?

HUSBAND:    I'm fine, there's nothing to worry about, seriously.

*HUSBAND's phone rings. He takes it.*

HUSBAND:    Hello? No I haven't. How serious is it? I see. I'll put it on right now.

VICTORIA:    Is something the matter at the Ministry?

HUSBAND:    I'm afraid so.

*By now they're in the kitchen and HUSBAND puts the TV on. The public channel comes up and a news commentator is running through the day's headlines.*

JOURNALIST:    John Mahoney, of *The Radical Daily*, is making some serious claims. Apparently, according to what he has published in his column today, he has in his possession documents, including reports, fiscal receipts, invoices, private emails and phone call recordings that involve the Minister of Finance, a number of contractors and high-level civil operators, giving clear evidence of abuse of state funds, unabashed conflict of interest, infringement of EU tendering laws, exploitation of power and the falsification of reports and documents read in parliament. The accusations seem to be catastrophic…

*HUSBAND switches the TV off and starts for the door.*

VICTORIA:     Is this true?

HUSBAND:     True or not, people will believe it.

VICTORIA:     Don't let them tarnish your name. Whatever happens, whatever they're saying, you've got nothing to do with this.

HUSBAND:     I know, but whatever it is I'm the one that has to answer for it. I'll talk to you later, okay?

VICTORIA:     Call me as soon as you can and let me know how I may help.

HUSBAND:     I will, I promise.

VICTORIA:     Don't forget we have to attend my brother's soirée this evening.

HUSBAND:     Oh yes, there's that, I won't forget. Good day.

VICTORIA:     God bless you.

*HUSBAND leaves closing the door loudly behind him. VICTORIA turns to the coffee still on the kitchen counter realizing that HUSBAND hasn't touched it.*

VICTORIA:     I'll be fine he said. And he'll be fine too. I'm sure of it. Won't we, Lord? We'll be both fine.

*VICTORIA smiles.*

BLACKOUT

04

ONSCREEN – THE TALK

JOURNALIST & BROTHER

JOURNALIST:     I hope you do not take this as an inappropriate question, but considering the circumstances, it is a question I believe one cannot overlook. Would you agree, Dr Buhagiar, that given your families' history, apart from her religious beliefs your sister might have also had a strong political opinion?

BROTHER:     Well, this question is truly one which cannot be neglected. We come from a family that has been affiliated with the

Christian Democratic Party for over four generations. Our own father, as the entire country knows, was leader of the party and Prime Minister of this nation. I have been elected member of the European Parliament on a party ticket, and so the question is obviously out there in everybody's mouth, what does this mean for Victoria politically? Let me tell you the truth. As hard as it is to believe, Victoria had no partisan political stands at all. Victoria only had Christ; Christ and the Bible. It wasn't Victoria who leaned towards politics, it was politics that leaned towards Victoria. All of us saw in her a guiding voice, a light. Everything Victoria has ever done has always been to keep our island, our country, a truly strong and virtuous Christian nation. Our party is a Christian Democratic Party, it is in our very nature to follow our Christian hearts, our Christian roots. Then how could we not follow Victoria?

CUT TO JOURNALIST & HUSBAND

JOURNALIST:          We would like to get to know Victoria from a closer perspective, the way she was at home, maybe even when she was younger. How did you meet her? Did you date? Was dating Victoria like dating a normal person?

HUSBAND:     The first time I noticed Victoria was in church. I must have been twenty-two years old, yes, I was twenty-two and she was twenty. I remember she was singing with the parish prayer circle girls' choir and she was up front, on the stand to the right of the altar at the parish, St. Paul's Church. I guess I noticed her and took a fancy but it was weeks before we actually met in person and spoke to each other. She was responsible for a young Catholics youth committee in the locality and I started attending her meetings and joined the group, to get close to her of course. But before long she had me knee-deep in projects and fundraising activities and organizing volunteer work. You know Victoria, she was always like that, work, work, work; yet we did get closer and after a while both of us realized that we make a good team so we decided to take the relationship further.

JOURNALIST:     Was Victoria always a religious woman?

HUSBAND:     Since as long as I can remember her. And not only pious, Victoria was truly devoted and committed to the cause. She would not spend a single minute of her waking life on anything that could not in some way or other have an evangelical root or purpose. For Victoria every job, every instant, was an opportunity to work for the Lord. That was her higher calling. I believe she answered.

05

ONSTAGE

*DOWNSTAGE LEFT now has a small office setup; a desk and two chairs. VICTORIA is interviewing a potential INTERN.*

VICTORIA:     So why do you want to work here?

INTERN:     I just finished my degree in media and publishing, so now I need to get some real life experience in the industry. This would be a great opportunity for me / to learn about…

VICTORIA:    What do you think we do here Lydia?

INTERN:    You publish two magazines, right?

VICTORIA:    No. Not at all. If we published two magazines it wouldn't be me here, right now, sitting behind this desk. It would be someone else running this place. I wouldn't put all my life's work, commitment and faith in publishing two magazines.

INTERN:    Sorry, I'm not understanding…

VICTORIA:    Of course you're not understanding. You can't understand. You've just spent three to four years at that brothel they call a university. All you can understand are pagan words because they siphoned out of you all the words they don't want you to understand ever again. Once you've walked through these doors though Lydia, once you've walked in here, you've walked into another world, a world that means something deeper, something of actual, real significance. What we do here matters more than anything else happening out there. Try again. Take a look at this. What are you holding there in your hands?



*VICTORIA puts the latest two issues of her magazines in the INTERN's hands. The INTERN looks at them with a befuddled expression.*

INTERN:     These are the two latest issues of your magazines, *Iesus* and *Sagra Familia*.

VICTORIA:     You are still using the words they taught you at university…

INTERN:     I'm sorry Mrs. Sultana, / I can't…

VICTORIA:     What you're holding there, in your hands, Lydia, is the WILL of GOD. The. Will. Of. God. Lydia. This is what we do here and only this. Nothing more and nothing less. This is my calling, and the calling of every single human being I deem worthy of being part of this endeavour. At every single step in the carving and the weaving of this work, we make sure, guarantee, that all of it, from the typing of the first words to the pictures we put in it and the businesses that advertise on it—every single tiny step that makes these two *receptacles* come into existence—is only and exactly what God wants, and what

God is willing into being. See why I can't have just anybody working here? Do you think that a person who is unable to recognize the Will of God when holding it in their very bare hands is actually worthy of committing their mind, body and soul to becoming a part of that very Will?

INTERN:  I think I'm understanding better now what you mean. It is very important for your staff to be dedicated to the mission statement / of this enterprise…

VICTORIA:  Did what I just tell you sound like a mission statement to you? Is that what you think I'm doing right now? Teaching you our "mission statement"?

INTERN:  Well, I think, / I'm only trying to…

VICTORIA:  When was the last time you prayed Lydia?

INTERN:  Sorry?

VICTORIA:  Prayer. When was the last time you knelt in prayer and prayed to the Lord for the sake of your soul and the souls of your loved ones?

INTERN:         I'm not the praying type Mrs.
                Sultana.

VICTORIA:       I figured as much. So let's
                reschedule another appointment and make
                a small plan. You take with you *Iesus* and
                *Sagra Familia* today, take some time to
                understand better what we do here, and let
                these words help you find your path back to
                prayer. And then we'll meet again to see if
                you're better prepared to become a partner
                in God's Will.

INTERN:         I thought / maybe…

VICTORIA:       In three weeks' time, is that good for
                you?

INTERN:         I should be free, I guess…

VICTORIA:       Perfect. See you in three weeks then.

INTERN:         Thank you…for your time.

VICTORIA:       God bless you dear.

EXIT INTERN

## 06

ENTER SECRETARY

SECRETARY:   So, when is she starting?

VICTORIA:   I doubt she'll ever be starting but I'm giving her a second interview in three weeks for the benefit of the doubt.

SECRETARY:   She was sent here by Madam First Lady herself. You're expected to employ her.

VICTORIA:   Madam First Lady knows I don't do favours. If she wants to find the girl a job she should have put her in charge of one of her thousand charities. Anyway, don't waste your time worrying about any of that. I'll deal with Madam First Lady. Have the writers all handed in their anti-divorce pieces for our next issue?

SECRETARY:   Yes madam, it's all being proofread as we speak.

VICTORIA:   Good. That's everything for now.

SECRETARY:   Thank you madam.

VICTORIA:   Oh, has my husband called by any chance?

SECRETARY:  No madam, you did not have any
calls.

VICTORIA:     Do let me know if he does.

EXIT SECRETARY

07

*VICTORIA picks up her mobile phone from the inside of her
jacket which is hung on the chair behind her desk. She dials
and waits. No reply. VICTORIA doesn't leave a message. She
puts the phone back in her jacket, gets her office desk phone
and dials.*

VICTORIA:     May I speak to Mr. George Sultana
please. —This is Mrs. Sultana. —*long pause*—
What do you mean he's not in today? —May
I speak to his colleague then? —May you
please tell Mr Camilleri that Victoria Sultana
is waiting on the phone. —*long pause*—Hi
John. —That's why I'm calling, I'm having
difficulty getting a hold of him too. He's not
at the Ministry? —Sick? Are you sure that's
exactly what his message said? —And when
was this? —I see. I'll make sure to pass him
the message. —Good day to you too.

*VICTORIA puts the phone back down and stares into the empty space ahead of her. Snippets of earlier conversations start coming back to her in voiceover.*

HUSBAND (V.O.):     Listen, I was thinking, why don't we go on a little holiday? Pack a little suitcase each and disappear for a couple of days?—You'll do fine Victoria. I know you will. Everything will be fine.—I know you won't give up.

*As VICTORIA hears these words playing over and over again we can see a red stain appearing on her white blouse, on her right side, just below her ribs. Then she feels a sharp pain and falls to the floor on her knees. She's holding her side where the stain has appeared and with her other hand she grabs the wastebasket from underneath the desk and pulls it towards her. She throws up violently.*

*Her SECRETARY walks in alarmed. VICTORIA stays on the floor buckled over in front of the wastebasket with hand outstretched to keep her SECRETARY away from her. Her SECRETARY tries to come close to help but VICTORIA pushes her away.*

SECRETARY:  Madam!

VICTORIA:     I'm fine! Don't touch me.

SECRETARY:  But…

VICTORIA:     I said I'm fine! Just give me a minute.
              This will pass.

*Her SECRETARY runs out. VICTORIA puts the
wastebasket away and sits up against her desk. She removes a
glove and puts a hand inside her blouse to examine her side.
She winces when she touches herself and the hand comes back
out all bloody. Then she looks at her palm and a look of horror
passes over her face. She removes the other glove and looks at
both her palms. Each one is extremely sore with blood oozing
out of them. She lifts both palms up as if showing them to God.*

VICTORIA:     Oh Lord, why today? Why does it
              have to be today?

*Her SECRETARY comes back holding a glass of water but is
immediately shocked as soon as she sees VICTORIA sitting
on the floor with both hands upturned and bloody. As soon as
VICTORIA notices her presence she puts her gloves back on
and stands up, regaining some composure. Throughout the
rest of this dialogue, she's putting on her jacket and packing
her things to leave the office.*

SECRETARY:   I thought you might need a glass of
              water.

VICTORIA:     No thanks, I'm fine, I don't need
              anything.

SECRETARY:   But it's just some water…

VICTORIA:     Why are you tempting me so? You
              know what I live on; the Word of God, and
              the Body and Blood of Christ. That's all I
              need. I already heard Mass this morning
              before coming to the office, my nourishment
              has already been taken care of so I don't need
              anything else to sustain me. I just need to rest
              a little and I'll be fine. I'm going home, I'll
              continue my work from there.

SECRETARY: I'll postpone the rest of your
              appointments for the day.

VICTORIA:     Yes please, and pray do keep this
              episode private.

SECRETARY:  I understand madam, but, excuse my
              forwardness, I don't mean to offend, but
              don't you think it would be wise to see a
              doctor?

VICTORIA:     My experiences, Suzanne, are not
              experiences that may be understood by just
              anyone and people tend to misinterpret what
              they don't understand. Misinterpretations
              give rise to confusion, ignorance and lies. My
              work here is to execute the Will of God, and
              it is my responsibility to ensure that the Will

of God is never entangled in confusion, ignorance and lies. So, do you understand, Suzanne, why it might not always be wise to see a doctor?

SECRETARY:   I understand. I'm sorry.

VICTORIA:     No need to be sorry. All you need is faith—faith and more faith. God bless you dear.

EXIT VICTORIA

*SECRETARY makes the sign of the cross and starts to sob.*

BLACKOUT

08

ONSCREEN – THE TALK

JOURNALIST & FAMILY DOCTOR

JOURNALIST:           As their family doctor for how long have you been tending to Victoria?

FAM. DOCTOR:         I have been their main general practitioner practically all their lives. I have followed their father, God rest his soul, up until his last days and I have also seen Victoria since she was a child.

JOURNALIST: As her doctor were you ever made aware of Victoria's wounds in her palms and feet?

FAM DOCTOR: Yes, I was asked to consult quite some time ago but they weren't always wounds, at first Victoria only had sores and if I'm not mistaken the first time her sores were brought to my attention was when Victoria was fourteen years old. She had rosy round sores on both her palms and feet, and she complained of constant itching and sometimes burning pain. Her mother had informed me that all four sores appeared over three weeks, first starting with a sore on one hand and then gradually appearing on the other hand and both feet. I was contacted only once the four sores had all appeared and, according to her mother, after all the regular over-the-counter skin ointments did not bear any form of effect. The sores seemed to flare and subside at irregular intervals; sometimes they were damp and almost bleeding but on occasions they became extremely dry and started to flake off skin. I tried to diagnose her condition for over a year, and I also involved dermatologists, but no diagnosis was ever satisfactory and no cure ever worked. We performed enough tests to eliminate all possible sources; it wasn't an allergy, she had no signs of infection such as an accompanying fever or other signs of illness, all tests for bacterial or viral infections came back negative and all blood and urine sample tests were found completely clean.

JOURNALIST: Have you ever observed signs of foul play on the young Victoria or been given reason to believe that her sores, as you are describing them, might have been physically self-inflicted?

FAM DOCTOR: No, if the sores were self-inflicted there would have been clear signs such as accidental puncture wounds in the skin or unevenness in the formation of the rash, and over a period of time there would have definitely been some form of infection. I believe it is near impossible to nurture, so to speak, an open wound via physical means without your wound becoming infected in some way or other. Victoria's wounds never exhibited any of the regular signs of infection. Ultimately, my decision, with Victoria and her family, was to stop looking for a cure or a diagnosis and to focus on making the experience as relatively painless as it could be.

JOURNALIST: How long had you been trying to diagnose or cure Victoria's wounds?

FAM DOCTOR: For approximately two years, but throughout that time Victoria seemed to grow accustomed to her condition. She almost started to become reluctant to find a cure.

JOURNALIST: So you gave these sores a religious or divine interpretation?

FAM DOCTOR: At first I was very hesitant to do so and I did my utmost to discover a medical explanation to the appearance of those sores, but it was very clear that over time Victoria herself was becoming more and more religious both in nature and in her own interpretation of her wounds. I believe that it was for that very reason that she became averse to the idea of curing her sores.

There must have been a point were Victoria started believing in the possibility that her wounds were a blessing and not a curse.

JOURNALIST:                    But what about your beliefs Doctor? Did you ever stop believing that there was a medical explanation or a medical origin to Victoria's wounds?

FAM DOCTOR:        Soon after Victoria's own change of heart with regard to her condition her father, as you all know, fell seriously ill. That's when he became my major concern in the family. Victoria seemed to be more or less stable and coping. She took very good care of her hands and feet, and we all became used to her gloves. Her father's illness was a much more public and high profile affair given his political stature and I was a big part of all that, so for many years I didn't give much thought to Victoria's wounds. My hunch was always that Victoria must have been suffering from some kind of rare genetic skin condition, something we couldn't actually test for or diagnose with our available resources, and that's what I thought for many years up until the more recent events.

JOURNALIST: So your opinion changed recently?

FAM DOCTOR: Yes, my opinion did change. This happened when I was called by her mother on the day of Victoria's passing. I still cannot understand what I saw that day. It wasn't just the wounds on her palms and feet; Victoria was suffering an excruciating amount of pain on the day she died. I truly have stopped trying to explain it. All I can say is that for my entire Christian life I have been seeing the life and pain of Christ portrayed or explained to me; but I had never completely understood, nor entirely imagined, what kind of pain Jesus Christ could have truly experienced during the crucifixion. Not until that day, when I saw with my own eyes the physical condition of Victoria Sultana.

JOURNALIST: But did any detail strike you as particularly odd or supernatural?

FAM DOCTOR:     The whole experience was very overwhelming but yes there was something that disturbed me even further. Victoria had a number of bleeding open wounds which I had to dress, so I had to get close and was expecting the usual strong smell of blood, but there was no smell of blood at all. Instead, her wounds seemed to be emanating a delicate and sweet perfume. As she lay dying, Victoria literally smelled of flowers.

FADE TO BLACK

09

ONSTAGE

*VICTORIA enters her house, downstairs and stops at the foot of the staircase.*

VICTORIA:     George? George are you home?

*There's no answer. She runs upstairs to the bedroom and there's no one. Then she opens the wardrobe to find it half empty. She starts pulling drawers out of the armoire and the drawers she's pulling out are completely empty. All signs of HUSBAND have been removed from the bedroom. She sits on the edge of the bed and sobs. Taking hold of her crucifix in both her hands, she sobs, letting her tears fall on the prostrate Christ.*

*The phone rings and breaks her moment of misery. She wipes the tears from her face and picks up the phone from HUSBAND's side of the bed.*

VICTORIA:     George, is it you? Where are you?

*There's an uncomfortable pause before the other side answers.*

VICTORIA:     (*embarrassed*) Yes, yes, it is I. I'm sorry I thought you were someone else. — I'm sorry to disappoint you sir but no, he isn't.—The honest truth is that no, I do not. I do not know when my husband will be back and at the moment I have no way to reach him whatsoever.—No need to apologize. Good afternoon.

*VICTORIA stared at the phone in silence, trying to understand the call she just had but not even a single beat later the phone rings again. She takes the call.*

VICTORIA:     Hello?—Who's calling please?— No, unfortunately he isn't.—I'm sorry but at the moment I can't help you.—Yes, if I do I will let him know that *The Times* would like a statement, I understand.

*VICTORIA hangs up abruptly before the journalist can ask another question.*

VICTORIA:     Dear God, wheels are in motion. I can feel them turning. I know what wheels in motion feel like because on many occasions I was the one turning them. But not today. There's another hand at play today. Someone else is turning the wheels and all I can do is suffer the consequences. I know this because my wounds know this. My wounds are trying to tell me something. (*She removes her gloves and looks at the wounds on her palms. Blood drips from both hands.*) Something is approaching. Something is coming for me. What is it God? What is coming for me? I need help.

*Then she dials a number herself and waits for an answer.*

VICTORIA:     Brother, it's me, I have to ask you something.—Listen, have you seen or heard from George this morning? I can't seem to get him on the phone.—You're right, he must be busy with the scandal.—I'm sorry to have disturbed you. I just wanted to see how he's doing.—I'm fine, I'm totally fine, just over-reacting a bit. I don't know why I'm behaving like this. Do let me know if you get in touch with him though.—Yes of course. I'll see you at the party.

*VICTORIA puts the phone down and stares at the empty bedroom. She is still not convinced that any of this is normal.*

*She runs downstairs and goes out into the garden to the statue of the Virgin Mary. She hugs the statue and pushes her forehead against the forehead of the statue.*

VICTORIA:     Oh Holy Virgin, Queen of the Righteous, Mother of Grief, hear my prayers in this time of sorrow.

*VICTORIA tries to pray but voices from earlier keep entering her head.*

HUSBAND (V.O.):     Listen, I was thinking, why don't we go on a little holiday? Pack a little suitcase each and disappear for a couple of days?—You'll do fine Victoria. I know you will. Everything will be fine.—I know you won't give up.

SECRETARY (V.O.):     I thought you might need a glass of water.—but don't you think it would be wise to see a doctor?

VICTORIA (V.O.):     I'm fine, I'm totally fine…

A CLAP OF THUNDER

*Then we hear a loud clap of THUNDER and the sound of a HEAVY RAIN SHOWER. VICTORIA falls to her knees in front of the statue, her head stretched backwards with her face and hands open facing the sky. She screams the words —*

VICTORIA:      Father! May this cup be taken from me! Yet not my will be done; but yours!

*She tilts her head back violently as if an invisible hand pulled her hair. Her mouth is now wide open and she seems to be relishing water cascading down her throat.*

10

*By now VICTORIA's MOTHER has entered the house and is watching and hearing VICTORIA shout these words. MOTHER is visibly aghast at her daughter's behaviour. The sound of RAIN stops as soon as MOTHER runs out into the garden.*

MOTHER:      Victoria!

*VICTORIA breaks out of the trance and is both surprised and embarrassed at seeing her MOTHER standing there in her garden. But VICTORIA is also very weak, so she stumbles to the floor as she talks.*

VICTORIA:      Hello mother…Things, mother, things are happening…

MOTHER:      Good lord what have you done to yourself now! Look at you!

VICTORIA:     Why are you here? I didn't hear you walk in. Watch out, you'll get wet in the rain.

MOTHER:      *(looking up at the clear sky)* What rain?

VICTORIA:     The rain mother. Can't you feel it? It's raining, God has sent me rain, He wants me to drink it.

MOTHER:      I can't take more of this nonsense of yours. I've been calling you for over an hour! Why aren't you at the office? Everyone is looking for you!

VICTORIA:     For me? Why me? Why is everyone looking for me? Today of all days…

MOTHER:      You're not making any sense! Stand up and pull yourself together, we have to go, you've been summoned!

VICTORIA:     Yes, I know, the Lord, Mother, this is the day. The Lord is summoning me.

MOTHER:      The high committee has summoned you Victoria! An urgent emergency meeting has been called and madam First Lady wants you at the board hearing right now!

VICTORIA: Madam First Lady wants me right now? I hope this has got nothing to do with that hussy she wanted me to employ.

MOTHER: I don't know a thing, useless asking me. But you sure can't drive in this condition. I'll drive you there myself. Let's go. Everyone is waiting.

VICTORIA: Mother, why do I feel like something horrible is about to happen?

MOTHER: Victoria, you know our family has always been in the eye of the storm. We have made things happen in this country and things have happened to us. But never forget what your father always said: "Whatever happens, you can always come home and there will always be a family waiting." Now let's go, this will all be over very soon. Whatever it is.

VICTORIA: Amen to that.

BLACKOUT

## 11

ONSCREEN – THE TALK

JOURNALIST & FIRST LADY

JOURNALIST: Madam First Lady, you were the one to hire Victoria Sultana for the editorial position within your Christian publications. What made you hire Victoria?

FIRST LADY: I have known Victoria, by God's grace, since she was just a child because I am a good friend of her mother and I have always been close to their family. I have seen Victoria grow from an adorable little girl into this unbelievably strong and determined young woman. But unlike other young women, Victoria's ambition was never of this world. Her uncompromising faith, her devotion to Our Lord, is what convinced me that this young woman needed to be in a position where her example could be seen by everyone, where her words, her experience, her belief could move everyone. She was a teacher in a church school, already doing her best to cultivate a stronger faith in our future generations but I knew we could give her more than that. I knew Victoria deserved to be in a place where her inspiring devotion could literally reach everyone in this country, young and old. So that is exactly what we did.

JOURNALIST: Did her condition, her suffering, in any way influence your relationship with Victoria?

FIRST LADY: One could never look at Victoria in parts. Victoria was Victoria, her words, her strength, her faith, her pain; Victoria was one with the Lord all the time and we were always completely respectful of that. To be in her presence, especially during our prayer gatherings, felt like being in the presence of somebody who truly has a deeper experience of the Lord than we could ever have, but she shared that with us. She helped us not only understand our relationship with Our Lord better but also foster it, and nourish it, and I am sure that her pain was very much a big part of that. We always knew what she was going through, and we always did our best to help her and be by her side in her most difficult moments, right until her final hour.

JOURNALIST:    Did you visit Victoria on the day she passed?

FIRST LADY:   Yes, I did. I was informed by her mother that she was having a very severe episode and I immediately went to their home where I remained by Victoria's side with her family and their family doctor; I was there all day until Victoria, very unexpectedly, passed away in the evening.

JOURNALIST:    Can you tell us what happened that day?

FIRST LADY:   I can only talk about what I saw myself. I received the call at about noon and I was by her side by around one o'clock. Victoria was in bed and her mother was praying next to her. Her husband and her brother were also present and so was the doctor. Victoria seemed to be going through severe ecstatic bouts. She would begin to look into the space above her face, not at the ceiling, but at the air, as if there was something she was seeing there that we couldn't. And she would talk in whispers to whatever or whoever she was seeing. And then she would enter into moments of agony. At one point she started screaming in pain, and raise and open her arms wide to the side as if someone was stretching her hands, pulling them, as if she was being crucified, and all of us could actually see the holes in her arms widen and deepen and the blood gush out from them as if invisible nails were being hammered into her hands. I couldn't bear to watch. It was one of the most horrible things I have ever seen. The woman suffered terribly.

JOURNALIST: And did she at any point talk to you?

FIRST LADY: Yes, after her moments of agony she would always enter a deep sleep and then she would wake up lucid and ask for us one by one. She told us that the Virgin Mary was in great pain seeing the world become so rotten, so corrupt. She told us we need to pray for our country because it, too, is starting to rot. And I believe that this was why Victoria suffered the crucifixion; just like Jesus had suffered, for all of our sins, Victoria suffered for the sins of our country. Her agony and death are a sign to us all, a sign that shows us how much we need to change our ways, our lives, and how close to Jesus, to God, we need to return if we are to ever truly find salvation.

FADE TO BLACK

12

ONSTAGE

*DOWNSTAGE LEFT we see a long table with a number of very sombre people around it. VICTORIA is one of them. The man at the head of the table stands and starts reading from a letter. As the MAGISTRATE reads the letter we can see VICTORIA becoming more and more agitated.*

MAGISTRATE: Dear friends and colleagues, we are meeting here today under the watchful gaze and care of our Lord God almighty with the blessing of his Holiness the Pope and the Sovereign State of Malta to review the roles bestowed upon our sister Victoria Sultana in light of the contemporary social and cultural contexts within which we are operating today. With great enthusiasm, dedication and rigour Victoria Sultana has served the board in an exceptional manner as the editor of its most popular and invaluable publications, Iesus and Sagra Familia. It is through these publications that the board reaches out into the very minds and souls of the population ensuring the protection and promotion of our Catholic culture and Christian faith. Victoria Sultana has done this and more as editor-in-chief of our publishing house and for this we are showing her our most heartfelt gratitude by giving her a gift and offering her a new role to help us continue our most prestigious work in this country. The gift is a Mercedes-Benz luxury / sedan.

VICTORIA:    But I already have a car! (Whilst standing and interrupting rudely.)

*Everyone round the table looks at VICTORIA in embarrassment and disdain. There's a short uncomfortable silence.*

VICTORIA:    I'm sorry for interrupting sir, but I don't see the point. I already have a car. I don't need any gifts. I don't do God's work to receive gifts.

FIRST LADY:  Not now Victoria. Let him finish, we'll talk afterwards.

*VICTORIA sits back in her seat, nobody else comments, and the MAGISTRATE continues.*

MAGISTRATE:  The gift we are bestowing upon our sister Victoria, will supplement her new role; that of curator of our charity fund. Her function, should she willingly accept our offer, will be to receive and judge applications, visit the individuals or institutions in need and personally deliver the funds. This would be performed to the yearly salary of a hundred and sixty thousand euros pre-tax.

*VICTORIA stands up and interrupts again, with more conviction this time.*

VICTORIA:  I would like to thank this board for the offer being made to me here today but I sincerely believe that my mission as chief editor of these two publications is far from over and I still have a lot of contributions to give, especially considering the moral tests our country is about to face. There are people already waging war against our values, spreading terrible lies about the convenience of divorce and unholy marriages. God forbid, some even dare to talk of the murder of innocent children in the womb! My fight is surely far from over! I would like to discuss this issue with the bishop and seek his personal council before I accept any decision upon this matter.

*A PRIEST replies to her claims.*

PRIEST:	The bishop has already been made aware of these matters and he has given us his seal of approval right here in writing, both for your new appointment and for the appointment of your replacement.

VICTORIA:	So, this is it? You think you can all buy me off with a new car and a higher salary? What do you take me for?

FIRST LADY:	Mind your tone Victoria.

VICTORIA:	Gluttons, all of you! A pathetic club of nepotistic gluttons! No wonder this country is going to the dogs if even the ones supposed to lead it, to uphold its moral integrity, to see to the conservation of its values and beliefs, have turned into nothing but political lap dogs, willing to lick at every profitable passing wind!

FIRST LADY:    Enough! We won't have any of this! You drew first blood. You spat at the sky!

VICTORIA:    How?! When?! I've dedicated my whole life to what I believed was the mission of this council; to lead this country in the footsteps of Our Saviour, to be a constant witness for the teachings of Our Lord! Have I betrayed this council? Or has this council betrayed itself?

FIRST LADY:    You betrayed your friends Victoria. You betrayed all of us when you betrayed the Party. You think we don't know it was you? You think we cannot imagine who's behind the chaos we've had to face all day? The accusations? The conspiracies? The newspapers have been all over us since this morning! The Prime Minister is but in tears, holed up in his office clutching at straws, desperately calling in the worst sort of favours to claw himself out of the pit you dug for him!

VICTORIA:     What are you talking about? What accusations?

FIRST LADY:  Where is your husband Victoria? Where is he hiding?

VICTORIA:     What?! How do you…

FIRST LADY:  How do I what? How do I know he's hiding? Because that is what cowards do after stabbing their friends in the back. And we all know who your husband works for Victoria. We all know where his loyalty will forever stand, not by our side, not by any party, but by yours! Your husband works only for you!

VICTORIA:     There's a big misunderstanding here. There must be. I don't know what you are talking about, please, believe me…

FIRST LADY:  Believe you? You can't even start to believe yourself!

VICTORIA:     So why would I do all this? Humour me for a minute, after all these loyal years, why would I betray you now? What do I have to gain from all of this?

FIRST LADY:   We know how far you'd go for your convictions. You stopped seeing the forest for the trees years ago. You're always on about how we are becoming too soft, too materialist, too liberal. This must be your way of pushing us all out and bringing back in your own chosen one. The leader will not survive these scandals and you know it. Once in the clear, your husband will be back like nothing ever happened. And you already have somebody else lined up to take over the Party, you've been grooming him for years, and now it is finally happening. For all your talk of faith and God's Will you've always been a political animal. Did you believe we would not retaliate?

*VICTORIA is starting to feel light-headed and she can barely stand anymore.*

VICTORIA:   I'm looking for my husband; I'm looking for George. He left me. He packed his bags and left. You are all mistaken. I know nothing of this conspiracy. My husband left me today and I am looking for him, this is my story, this is my truth. I did not attack anybody, I did not betray anybody, I have not been grooming anybody. I cannot understand why this is happening to me today, oh dear God, dear Mother Mary, come to my help, open the eyes of my brothers and sisters here in this room, in the name of Jesus Christ, please, dear chairman, dear magistrate, please listen, believe me for what I say is the only truth.

*By now the whole table is whispering and pointing at VICTORIA.*

MAGISTRATE:	Good Lord, what's wrong with this woman?

FIRST LADY:	Victoria, I think you're bleeding from your gloves…

*VICTORIA raises her gloved hands to see a trickle of blood falling out of each glove and splattering on the table. The wound on her side has appeared again and more blood is seeping onto her blouse. The table is in commotion now and they are all coming closer to see what's happening to VICTORIA's hands. VICTORIA tries to walk away but she stumbles towards the middle of the room. She falls to her knees, removes her gloves and looks at the horrible wounds on both her palms. The small crowd looks aghast from over her shoulders.*

VICTORIA:     Please help me…I just need to find
              my George…If I find George I'm sure he'll
              explain everything…

A CLAP OF THUNDER

*Suddenly the onlookers grab VICTORIA and picked her up
off the floor. Two of them hold her arms outstretched in front
of her and another two rip-off her blouse violently.
VICTORIA screams.*

VICTORIA:     What are you doing to me? Let me
              go!

ANOTHER CLAP OF THUNDER

*VICTORIA is now terrified by her environment as if she has
found herself in a completely different place. We can hear the
sounds of crying and sobbing people, wails of pain, snaps and
cracks of whips as if we are in some torture chamber.*

VICTORIA:     No! Let me go! Where am I? I
              shouldn't be here! Please, no! Oh my God it's
              really happening!

*The PRIEST is now wielding an invisible whip, and mimes
whipping VICTORIA. We hear a very loud crack of a whip
and VICTORIA screams and twists as if her back has just
been truly whipped.*

VICTORIA:     Please stop! Please! Aaahh!

*Another loud crack and VICTORIA screams and howls, as the whipping continues one lashing after another.*

*The group jeers and jests at VICTORIA. She begs for help, but everybody is enjoying the spectacle.*

VICTORIA:     Please, George, help me! I can't take it! It hurts so much! Where are you George? Please come back.

*Then the MAGISTRATE interjects-*

MAGISTRATE:          Crown him! He's the King isn't he? Then crown him, may he be honoured for the king that he is!

*The FIRST LADY comes to her holding a Crown of Thorns and as VICTORIA screams in horror, the FIRST LADY pushes the Crown of Thorns onto her head.*

EVERYBODY:          Hail the King of Jews! Hail the King of Jews!

*Blood seeps out of VICTORIA's head and covers her face. VICTORIA gives one long final howl of horror and falls to the ground.*

BLACKOUT

## End of Act One

## Interval

# Act Two

13

ONSCREEN – THE TALK

JOURNALIST & EXORCIST

JOURNALIST:        Father, you are the church's official exorcist here on the island and any supernatural occurrence falls within your expertise, am I correct?

EXORCIST:    That is true indeed. I'm the "go-to," so to speak in all of these mysterious cases.

JOURNALIST:        Over the course of these past few weeks everybody has been brandishing the words "stigmata" and "stigmatist", especially with reference to the wounds Victoria Sultana is said to have exhibited. Could you please explain to us what a stigmatist is and what the stigmata are?

EXORCIST:    Stigmatists are rare people that devote themselves so much to Jesus Christ, they get to share in His Passion. The most common type of experience they go through

is the suffering of the Five Holy Wounds of
Jesus Christ, also known as the Five
Stigmata. These are the wounds made by the
nails the Romans drove through Christ's
body to crucify him on his cross, one in each
palm and two through the feet. The fifth
mark is the wound to the side made by the
centurion who drove the spear into Christ's
left side, below the ribs, to ensure his death.
These are the Five Holy Wounds stigmatists
are said to suffer in likeness to the suffering
of Jesus on the cross. But experiences vary.

JOURNALIST:          Yes, this sort of extreme
experience definitely cannot be said to be
something regular or normal but there have
been recorded cases, historically speaking,
am I correct?

EXORCIST:     Yes, there have been a few. The most
famous ones are of course San Francesco
D'Assisi and Padre Pio di Pietrelcina.
Francesco, or as we call him Saint Francis,
was the very first stigmatist to have his
condition recorded by witnesses and his
story was depicted in detail by his
biographer. The story goes that Saint Francis

had a vision whilst he was on a pilgrimage and, in the vision, a crucified angel, a seraph we are told, appeared to him. His biographer describes how the moment was one of both extreme elation and extreme sadness and pain as Saint Francis empathized with the angel. It is this empathy that is said to have led the angel to pass on the marks of the crucifixion to the saint himself and from that moment onwards the saint exhibited the marks on his hands and feet and a deep wound at his side such as the one made on Christ with the centurion's spear. Yet Saint Francis' case is, obviously, not without controversy. First of all, one needs to consider the fact that there was nothing to stop his biographer from embellishing the story and we have to consider the era these writings come from. Here we have a biographer who is writing of such things back in the thirteenth century, an age when it was important for such writings to evoke emotional responses and impress the populace. The wounds of Saint Francis have been described as not only marks left in the palms and feet but as actual extensions in the shape of nails produced by a macabre malformation of the flesh. Such extreme descriptions could have possibly been exaggerated but this does not in any way impinge on our belief that Saint Francis suffered an extreme experience in relation to Christ's crucifixion.

JOURNALIST: But the case of Padre Pio is much more recent.

EXORCIST: Yes, it is, and due to it being a much more recent case, we have more detailed documentation. Padre Pio bore the signs of the stigmata for over forty years and his condition had been closely monitored and investigated by a few medical practitioners. No doctor was ever able to explain the wounds at his palms and feet, and the wounds never became infected. Some even said that his wounds smelled of flowers and he was said to suffer the entire passion of Our Lord on every Good Friday, with the passion starting from the previous Thursday and ending on Good Friday at three in the afternoon.

JOURNALIST: The hour Christ Himself is said to have died on the cross.

EXORCIST: Yes, the experience is said to have mirrored the one of Christ Himself as depicted in the Gospels.

JOURNALIST: And is it always priests that received the stigmata?

EXORCIST: No not at all, in fact the majority of known stigmatists have been women and some of them were married women. Not all of them have been declared Saints either, though some of course have. Again, stories vary. For example, Saint Catherine of Siena, of the Order of Saint Dominic back in the fourteenth century led an extremely interesting life, we have many writings of hers and she also had a biographer who described her own stigmatic phenomena. And there was Saint Catherine de Ricci, in the sixteenth century who was also reported to have experienced the stigmata. In the last century, we had cases such as the one of Marie Rose Ferron who died in 1936, Marthe Robin who died in 1982, and even more recently we had Evola Natuzzo, an Italian married woman who just died in 2009. Her case was followed by the Italian media and, as part of her stigmatic experience, she had words in Hebrew and Aramaic show up on her body as if written in blood on Good Friday and Easter Sunday. Her case is still under investigation.

JOURNALIST: Yet with all of these different cases and variations in mind, what would you say are the constant factors that might in one way or another bind all of these together?

EXORCIST: All of these people, whether male or female and whether ordained or not, have in their own manner dedicated their entire life to being witnesses for Our Lord here on Earth. All of them show an enormous devotion to the saints and to Jesus and all of them have led a life of prayer and fasting, whilst having experienced immense physical pain in their devotion to Christ. Another characteristic is that their service to the church is always a selfless and revolutionary one; these are people that strive for their entire life to give and add and, in their own way, shine a stronger light on the glory of God in His church, on most occasions even by challenging its institutions. Many of them helped in building convents and creating new Orders and motivating new missions. These have all been men and women that gave their all for the church and for their faith in the Lord, including, ultimately, their health and life.

JOURNALIST: And would you say that Victoria Sultana appears to fit in this description?

EXORCIST: Well, as I have already explained before agreeing to this interview, I cannot comment directly on the case of Victoria Sultana since the investigation is still in its earlier stages. I do not want my opinion to influence the proceedings in any manner. Though I am at liberty to say one thing: if the results of our investigation show that Victoria's wounds could not have been in any way a hoax or produced in acts of physical self-harm, and if everything that we are hearing about the woman's deeds and devotion turns out to be incontestable, then there might be the possibility for Victoria to be considered as one of the church's holy women. But until the investigation is completed, this is all mere speculation.

FADE TO BLACK

14

ONSTAGE

*For all of ACT 2 the house set is now decorated to represent MOTHER's house, the Sultana estate. The structure is exactly the same as before but the furniture looks older and more expensive, contrasting with the previous humble décor of VICTORIA's house in ACT 1.*

*DOWNSTAGE LEFT HUSBAND and VICTORIA are sitting on the floor as if laying down watching the stars. They are happy. During the following sequence HUSBAND is silent and his movements can be played with a more surreal approach. VICTORIA is her normal self, she's the only one with lines in this sequence.*

VICTORIA:     Thank you George. Thank you for the wonderful wedding, for bringing me here, for everything.

*HUSBAND puts his head in her lap and presses his face against her abdomen fondly. She's surprised and isn't sure what to do with the gesture. But she quickly relaxes and puts her gloved hands on his head caressing it.*

VICTORIA:     A family. You are right. That's what a married couple should do. Try to build a family.

*HUSBAND stands up and starts taking his clothes off. VICTORIA stops him.*

VICTORIA:     Do we have to try now?

*He approaches her slowly and tries to unbutton her blouse. VICTORIA stops him.*

VICTORIA:     I can't do this George.

*He kisses her on the lips and brings her body closer to his, clearly with more passion than their usual interactions.*

VICTORIA:     No please.

*She pushes him away. HUSBAND approaches again but she's quick to hold him back.*

VICTORIA:     No! George, why are you doing this to me? You know I can't be like this. It burns. Everywhere you touch me burns. My body is not for you. It's not even for myself. I can't just give it away because it is not mine, not anymore. Maybe children are not for us.

Maybe God has other things in store, but not this.

*HUSBAND is clearly enraged, he's clenching his fists, head bowed down, tears streaming down his face. He very quickly grabs her again and puts his mouth to hers but she reacts in convulsions. Her body becomes limp and he tries to hold her but she is having an attack in his arms. He gently lowers her to the ground where she stops moving and becomes very rigid, as if she's stretching herself from head to toes in polar directions. Then she sits up straight and starts speaking in tongues very loudly. It sounds like a language, but it is nothing recognizable, just loud sounds that could be a sequence of words in a sentence of an unknown language. HUSBAND is terrified. He kneels besides her and tries to get her attention but she keeps talking in the weird language as if he wasn't even there. Weeping, he holds her hand, as slowly her words become softer and she stops. VICTORIA collapses unconscious. HUSBAND picks up VICTORIA and takes her upstairs to the bedroom.*

BLACKOUT

15

*VICTORIA is in bed asleep. HUSBAND is sitting on the bed besides her, addressing her.*

HUSBAND:     Why you? Why does it have to be you to suffer so much? I thought I could do it, be with you and suffer with you for all our lives but I can't. That's the simple truth. I can't see you do it anymore. I can't be there to see you suffer anymore. And yet, by not being there, I shall myself inflict on you the worst suffering possible. You have no idea how sorry I am, but I just can't fight it. I can't fight these urges and these needs and desires any longer. I am weak Victoria. I am a weak man. And I am going to do terrible things only so that I may find some solace. Maybe God has not given me the strength you have. Or maybe I am simply done with God and His plans. I'm surrounded by men that make plans up everyday Victoria. Every day other men make plans for me, tell me what to do and ask me to follow blindly. And then I come home and you tell me to follow blindly God's plan. That it is all God's Will. Well, what about my plan? What about my will? Why does it have to be either other men or God? Why not me? I'm sorry that this has to hurt you so much, but believe me when I say that I'm not doing this out of spite and only because there truly is no other way. Goodbye Victoria.

EXIT HUSBAND

*VICTORIA wakes up suddenly, sweaty and feverish, clutching at the bed as if rising from underwater, gasping for air.*

VICTORIA:     George? Is that you? George?

BLACKOUT

16

ONSCREEN – THE TALK

JOURNALIST & HUSBAND

JOURNALIST:     Are there any particular moments from Victoria's last day that will remain forever with you more than others?

HUSBAND:     I was called by her mother, they were both in Victoria's office, and her mother called me and told me to come quickly because there was something wrong with Victoria. I left the meeting I was in at the Ministry and I went immediately to her office. Her mother was waiting for me outside and we entered Victoria's office together. I will never, never forget how we found her that day.

JOURNALIST:          Would you describe it for us?

HUSBAND:     Victoria was kneeling, in the middle of the room, with her head bowed in front of the crucifix. She was quiet, immobile, hands together with the rosary beads hanging from them. And the first thing I noticed was that she wasn't wearing her gloves. Then I started to follow a small rivulet of blood trailing down the rosary beads and falling on the floor right in front of her knees. I called her name, I didn't want to startle her but at the same time I wanted to see if she needed my help so I called her name and I approached her in the room and as I got closer she raised her head and looked at me. Her face was stained in tears of blood. Then her eyes literally turned upwards and all I could see was the whites of them. She fell to the floor unconscious and after a few seconds she came to again and it was as if nothing had happened. Her wounds stopped bleeding, her tears of blood stopped as well and she asked us why we were looking at her so strangely.

JOURNALIST: And that was when you took her home?

HUSBAND: Yes, she was very weak and since we didn't know if she was going to have another episode or not, her mother and I decided to take her home. Thank God we did because she started having another similar episode as soon as we arrived.

JOURNALIST: My question is, and many are wondering the same thing, why didn't you take her to a hospital?

HUSBAND: And tell them what? That she was crying blood and bleeding from her holy wounds? You have to understand that this was a very abnormal situation, one is never prepared for these things. It is also a fact that as her husband I was somewhat used to seeing Victoria exhibiting certain extreme behaviours and then returning to her normal self only within minutes. We also wanted to respect Victoria's wishes. She made it clear, in the moments when she was lucid, that she wanted to stay with her family at home. We thought that taking her to hospital when she was unconscious would be a betrayal.

JOURNALIST: You just mentioned that when her mother called, you were attending a meeting at the Ministry. Wasn't this the day that the Finance Ministry scandal broke in the news?

HUSBAND: Yes, it was. In fact, that was exactly what we were discussing in the meeting.

JOURNALIST: Were you directly involved in that situation?

HUSBAND: It is impossible for me not to be involved in such a situation; I am one of the highest-ranking officials in the Ministry. Though I would please ask you to refrain from asking me questions with regards to that case since it is still under investigation and as you all know I myself am also under investigation so I am bound by law not to speak publicly about the matter.

JOURNALIST: But could this situation at the Ministry in any way have affected Victoria?

HUSBAND: Why? Because she happened to be my wife?

JOURNALIST:            Because she herself had her own ties with the Party in government.

HUSBAND:    That has got nothing to do with what happened to Victoria that day. I was at a meeting and I left to be by the side of my suffering wife. My work at the Ministry had nothing to do with Victoria and I do not understand the necessity for this line of questioning which is being made by too many people in the media. Victoria's suffering and death had nothing to do whatsoever with party politics. Considering the virtues of the woman we're speaking of here, I find the insinuation rather ridiculous and offensive.

CUT TO JOURNALIST & BROTHER

JOURNALIST:            When did you hear that your sister was having another, shall we call it "episode"?

BROTHER:    My mother called me right after she called Victoria's husband, George, and I was on my way to Victoria's office when they called me again and told me that they were taking her to our mother's home, so I met them there.

JOURNALIST: So, when you arrived it was already happening?

BROTHER: No, since I was already on the road, I made it home first so they found me waiting for them. They arrived soon in George's car, my mom with Victoria at the back, so I went to help Victoria out of the car because she was visibly very weak and she started to pause as we walked towards the house. All of us noticed how she wasn't herself. I asked her if there's anything wrong, but she didn't reply and she slowly started to descend into a kneeling position right in front of the main door. George told us not to touch her, to give her space, and very gently he started to call her name but she didn't respond, she was in another place altogether. Then she raised her face and her eyes were rolled up inside her head so that all we could see were the whites and she started to pray, or that's what we think it was; it was a chant-like prayer in a different language, it was something that none of us could understand but it clearly sounded like prayer. To this day, none of us know what she said. Then she gave a shocking scream and collapsed. That was when George picked her up quickly in his arms and we took her inside.

JOURNALIST: It must have been a harrowing experience.

BROTHER: It was. I was aware that on some occasions my sister exhibited such episodes, both my mother and George had told me of occasions when they had witnessed moments such as these…but I was never present myself so that was the very first time I had seen my sister in such a state.

JOURNALIST: Would it be fair to say that you and your sister had a close relationship? She is the one who has always been by your side and who has always supported you in your political career, am I right?

BROTHER: Yes, that's true. I am sure that if it weren't for my sister I would definitely not be where I am today.

JOURNALIST: Had you ever discussed these episodes with her before that day?

BROTHER: Yes, I had. Victoria described both her wounds and her episodes as a sign and a blessing. For Victoria it was all a sign that her faith was true and that her mission was truly God's Will. She was happy that she received such an opportunity to live with Christ's pain in her life.

JOURNALIST: And weren't you ever worried for her health?

BROTHER: Of course, we were worried. All of us were concerned for her health and we couldn't not comment about the dangers of her fasting and her episodes of bleeding and speaking in tongues that she exhibited from time to time. When she was younger, she always asked for medical attention and our doctor had attended to her for many years. Though, as she grew older, she seemed to accept her condition more and more, and lately she started giving it an entirely new interpretation. At the end of the day, we all knew that she was a very special woman and that we were living in the presence of somebody who was graced with the presence of Our Lord in a way that most of us are not.

JOURNALIST:       Dr. Buhagiar, as I am sure you are well aware, the investigative journalist and blogger, Mariella Spiteri, has declared that she has conducted an independent inquiry into that fateful day which gives a completely different account of the events you and your family are claiming to have transpired. How do you react to these claims?

BROTHER:    To be honest, I was not surprised one bit. Mrs. Spiteri has made a career out of attacking my sister for her faith and devotion. A self-confessed atheist with no scruples whatsoever would not hesitate to stoop so low as to attempt to tarnish Victoria's reputation by exploiting this tragedy.

JOURNALIST:       But what about the witnesses she claims to have interviewed which gave evidence of a different timeline of events for how Victoria died?

BROTHER:     It's all a lie, a perverted fiction. None
             of Mrs. Spiteri's claims may be corroborated
             by anybody because her so called witnesses
             are all anonymous. Who are these people?
             What have they really seen? Why don't they
             come out and make their statements public
             instead of giving them to this so-called
             journalist? And even if she publishes her
             version of events like she is threatening to
             do, it will be nothing more than a fiction, a
             lie, a macabre fantasy she herself has
             invented to take one last stab at my sister's
             life and work. Mariella Spiteri should be
             ashamed of herself.

FADE TO BLACK

17

ONSTAGE

*VICTORIA is again in bed and she repeats the action and line
at the end of scene 16. VICTORIA wakes up suddenly,
sweaty and feverish, clutching at the bed as if rising from
underwater, gasping for air.*

VICTORIA:     George? Is that you? George?

*VICTORIA looks at her surroundings, then finds the switch
of a bedside lamp right next to her and puts it on.*

VICTORIA:     Are you here God? You are. I know
          you are. This, this is my childhood bed. I'm
          at Mother's, aren't I? How did I get here?
          Was George really here? Or was that just a
          dream? I could feel him so close. He was so
          sad. In such despair. He needs me, maybe
          even more than I need him. Where is he now
          God? Was he just in my dreams? Am I
          awake now? Prayer, I need to pray.

*VICTORIA gets slowly out of bed and kneels.*

VICTORIA:     The Lord is my light and my
          salvation; whom shall I fear? The Lord is the
          strength of my life; of whom shall I be afraid?
          When the wicked, even mine enemies and
          my foes, came upon me to eat up my flesh,
          they stumbled and fell. Though a host
          should encamp against me, my heart shall
          not fear: though war should rise against me,
          in this will I be confident. One thing have I
          desired of the Lord, that will I seek after; that
          I may dwell in the house of the Lord all the
          days of my life, to behold the beauty of the
          Lord, and to enquire in his temple. For in the
          time of trouble he shall hide me in his
          pavilion: in the secret of his tabernacle shall

he hide me; he shall set me up upon a rock. And now shall mine head be lifted up above mine enemies round about me: therefore will I offer in his tabernacle sacrifices of joy; I will sing, yea, I will sing praises unto the Lord.

*As she prays MOTHER & BROTHER walk up the stairs and stop to eavesdrop outside her bedroom door.*

MOTHER:     Do you think she's awake?

BROTHER:     Yes, yes, I'm sure I heard her voice.

*They open the door and interrupt her prayer.*

MOTHER:     Victoria, are you awake? How are you feeling?

VICTORIA:     I'm much better now, but why are you asking? What happened? How come I'm here?

BROTHER:     Mother was waiting for you outside the council meeting, they said you had some kind of strange fit, then you fainted. They helped you in Mother's car and she brought you home.

MOTHER:     I wanted to take you to hospital but you told me not to, dear.

VICTORIA:     I talked to you?

MOTHER:     Yes, as I put you in the car you were conscious, I was about to take you to the hospital and you asked me not to, you said you just wanted to sleep and then we'll make a proper appointment for a check-up later. I thought it was a sensible thing to do and since you were talking to me and seemed just a little weak, I agreed and brought you here.

BROTHER:     Why don't you come downstairs and have something to eat and drink, that is all you need, just something to eat and a little drink, maybe some water or a tea, it will bring you back your strength, you'll see.

MOTHER:     Your brother is right Vicky, come downstairs with us.

VICTORIA:     What time is it?

MOTHER:     It is almost eight. We still have an hour before the guests start arriving for the party. But don't worry, we have everything ready. Come down with us, you'll feel better soon.

VICTORIA:     I'll come, but promise you won't make me drink or eat anything. You know I don't do that.

BROTHER:     As you wish.

*In the kitchen downstairs, a small group of caterers and waiters are buzzing around making the final preparations for the foods. The garden outside is decorated with lights and the tables are set with candles. One table has three wine glasses, MOTHER goes to pick the wine glasses up and takes them to the kitchen.*

VICTORIA:     How many people are you expecting tonight Pierre?

BROTHER:     It depends; if everybody attends we might have around three hundred people...If everybody keeps his word, you know how they are. But this is an important time; things are happening, very shortly we will be on top of everything once again.

VICTORIA:     I thought we already were on top of everything.

BROTHER:     Not like this Victoria. Never like this! Our father left us a legacy we cannot ignore. I took some big decisions lately and to my own amazement, even though the decisions were the hardest I ever had to take, it all feels so natural. It is only now that I truly feel like I'm acting out my destiny.

VICTORIA:     The destiny our father laid out for you?

BROTHER:     Yes, exactly.

VICTORIA:     Pierre, when he was alive, our father kept you in the dark all the time. He sent you to schools abroad, made sure you were kept busy and out of sight, and he never let you in on anything. You know all this; you were always angry at him and frustrated because of how he treated you. And now you say he left you a legacy and you are taking charge? I don't understand Pierre. I thought that I was the one who took care of you after Father was gone. It was me who gave you all the support you needed and a vision to guide you.

BROTHER:    And I appreciate it and I love you dearly for everything you have done for me, sister. But now the times call for a different kind of politics, for a different kind of politician. I have much, much bigger plans now.

VICTORIA:    So, it is you. You are about to help remove our leader from office so you can take his place, isn't that your big plan?

BROTHER:    Shhhh! Slow down, lower your voice, even in here, you never know, somebody might be listening.

VICTORIA:    Answer my question, is that your plan?

BROTHER:    You are rushing, but yes, eventually, if everything works out and everybody plays his part, that is where I intend to be in a few months' time; at the helm of the country, on top of everything, right where our father was.

VICTORIA:    Have you considered the possibility that you are just another pawn? Isn't it obvious that you are being used by others who want to have their revenge on the Prime Minister for some reason or other?

BROTHER:     Of course, and what you are saying is very probable, but I do not have a problem with that. This is how things work. Everybody is in it for something, some of them are in it for the building permits and road contracts, and others have more personal motivations. But I do not see how that is my problem. My only problem is my goal and what needs to happen for me to achieve it. If enabling the twisted whims of others helps my success, then so be it, because I know that my success, in the long run, will be for the best. And I mean the best for everyone, not just us, but this entire country.

VICTORIA:     Today I was removed as editor of the Catholic publications and offered the management of some charity fund. How is that "for the best"?

BROTHER:     Well, to be completely honest that wasn't directly my fault, the board has been trying to find an excuse for ages and they finally did. But don't overreact about that, some change will do you good and I could surely help you manage those funds...

VICTORIA:    If you think that I am going to be part of your games Pierre, then you have no idea to whom you are talking to anymore. I will not be a part of this. This is nothing but a mess, a huge mess of backstabbing plots. I will have nothing to do with this corruption.

BROTHER:    Listen to me Victoria, listen closely. Once I'm where I should be, I will make sure you become chairperson of the High Office itself. I will be able to do that Victoria. You may choose whatever position you want, and I will make it happen. You will be a very powerful woman.

VICTORIA:    And I will refuse the appointment just like I will never touch their pathetic car. Is Mother aware of all this?

MOTHER:    Yes, dear?

*By now MOTHER has returned with two clean glasses and a bottle of wine. She pours a glass for BROTHER and herself and they are drinking.*

VICTORIA:    Are you in cahoots as well?

MOTHER:     This family has a name to live up to Victoria. We were never meant to live on the side or to be the moral compasses of those in charge. We were meant to *be* in charge. That is what your father has taught us, that is what he had achieved. Things are changing anyway. This current administration has its days numbered whether we do anything about it or not. They've been there for far too long. If your brother doesn't move in now, somebody else will and then it will all be over for us for good. You have to understand that what your brother is doing is what's best for the family, it is for all of us. I am sorry if all this hurts you, or if these methods go against your principles. In the long run you will realize that this was the best way forward.

VICTORIA:     I am beyond apologies mother. Apologies mean nothing. All I want now, the only single thing I want, is my husband back. You know about that, don't you? You know that George has left me.

BROTHER:     What do you mean Vicky? What do you mean George has left you?

VICTORIA: Oh, do not play dumb. That would be really, really cruel Pierre; faking it, lying some more to my face. You know what I mean. I was home earlier and George was gone. His things were not there and I can't talk to him. He made it look like he was going to work as usual, waited for me to leave and then turned back to get his things and go. That's the only sense I can make of it. I know he's the whistle-blower. I know he was the one who leaked everything to the journalists. And he must be helping you. There's no other explanation. You know everything, both of you. Where is he? Where is my George?

MOTHER: Please Victoria, calm down. This is not the time…

VICTORIA: I know that you know. I know that everybody knows. Everybody is hiding him away from me. Everybody is taking everything away from me because that is what their plans dictate, but what about me mother? What have you all done to me? Where is my George?

*VICTORIA says some of these words half-sobbing and MOTHER tries to console her with a hug but only a few seconds after, VICTORIA pulls back in disgust and she looks at the table.*

VICTORIA:     George was here. There were three wine glasses on the table when we arrived and that smell, I can smell him on you. He was here having wine with you just minutes ago, then he hugged you before he left.

BROTHER:     Stop it Victoria, now you are being paranoid and hysterical. We do not know where George is.

*VICTORIA breaks out into a rage.*

VICTORIA:     You are lying. You are lying. You know damn well where George is. He was here. George was here because of whatever it is you got him involved in. Tell me where he is. Tell me Pierre. Tell me now!

MOTHER:     Victoria, George has another woman.

*VICTORIA's sudden outburst quickly turns into disbelief and horror.*

BROTHER:     We didn't want you to find out like this, and he didn't either. But this is the truth.

He has been seeing somebody else and now he wants to leave with her and start a new life. The truth is he knew you would do everything in your power to stop him. George knew that the only way out of this marriage was escape. He is leaving the country tonight. Most probably he is on his way to the airport right now.

VICTORIA:   What? My George? But he can't just…

BROTHER:   Don't worry sister. Everything will be fine. We will take care of you.

VICTORIA:   You helped him, both of you. You helped my husband run away from me. You went to him for help. You needed someone from the inside, someone in the know for many years, to set up the Ministry of Finance fiasco and in return you helped him escape without me noticing. Most probably you even set him up with a job and a place to live wherever he is going with whoever she is; you, my brother and mother, my own family. How could you? How could you do this to me?

BROTHER:     I told you Victoria, I do whatever needs to be done. Though you are right with the story; that is basically what happened. But I did not go to George. He came to me. George was a sad and unhappy man Victoria; you never saw that, you were incapable of seeing that, you and your religious zeal, your insane fanaticism drove that poor man mad. You cannot judge him for what he did. He is still a good man.

VICTORIA:     Good man?! If what you're saying is true then he's nothing but a hypocrite and a coward!

*MOTHER tries to take VICTORIA's hand again to comfort her, but VICTORIA throws Mother's hand back at her before slapping her in the face. MOTHER just takes the slap, without a reaction, not even a cry. She just remains seated in silence and holds her face as VICTORIA walks away from them without another word. Across the stage, in the same position where there was previously the statue of the Virgin Mary, is now a big painting on an easel, a family portrait. Their father sitting on a red seat and the whole family by him, Mother, standing next to him and the children, brother and sister, by his feet. They look like royalty. VICTORIA stops in front of the portrait and BROTHER approaches her from behind.*

VICTORIA:   My whole world is collapsing around me. Could it be, could it be that for all this time, for my entire life, I was never doing God's bidding at all? Were I simply doing the bidding of others to satisfy their ends? And what if those ends were evil? Have I been corrupted and become evil too?

BROTHER:   No Victoria, you're not evil, not at all. But you have turned your back on us for far too long. You have betrayed us and betrayed yourself.

VICTORIA:   *I* have betrayed *you*?? After all of this, *I'm* the one who is to be accused of betrayal?!

BROTHER:   Yes, Victoria, you; you have betrayed our nature, you have betrayed your nature. Look at us there, look at what we were. Look at the beauty, look at the freedom, look at the power.

VICTORIA:   I refuse. I shall not place my sight upon such twisted and corrupt figures; we were monsters.

*BROTHER walks up closer and holds her from behind, he places his face against hers, his chin in her nape and hugs her. She shudders.*

BROTHER:     Look at us Victoria. Look at yourself. Where is the Victoria of that portrait? Where has she gone? I used to love her so much. We used to have so much fun together. The things we used to do Victoria. You were beautiful, wild, such a flame, such a passionate, uncaring flame. And then one day you were gone and all that was left of you was this; a shell of a woman full of nothing but fear, shame and disgust.

VICTORIA:     I am not ashamed of who I am, and I am only disgusted by you, my family. Yes, I did fear something once, I feared becoming another corrupt hypocrite. Today I only fear God.

BROTHER:     Oh no, it wasn't us you feared. It wasn't us you were ashamed of. It was yourself. I still remember you know; I still remember the things you made me do up in your room. The playful games you used to make me play. How deliciously twisted you were, even when so young!

VICTORIA:     Why are you saying these lies? I
              don't remember any of these lies, these
              disgusting lies, please Pierre. Stop. Stop this
              madness.

BROTHER:      These are not lies sister. These are
              memories. Memories you chose to be
              ashamed of. That's the only difference
              between you and I Victoria. I am not
              ashamed of who I am and what I did. You
              are. But all you did, my dear sister, was
              replace one monstrosity with another.

VICTORIA:     I am not the monster in this place. I
              am the truth, because Jesus does not lie;
              because my pain does not lie!

BROTHER:      I want to save you from that pain. I
              want to liberate you from your sickness,
              your madness. George told me everything;
              everything. Why did you do that to yourself?
              I cannot understand. I simply cannot. Why
              did you punish yourself so? Why do you
              keep putting on these fucking horrible
              gloves? Show me, show me what you did!

*Her BROTHER tries to remove her gloves but VICTORIA
resists and cries out. She falls to the ground but her*

*BROTHER is relentless. He grabs hold of her hands and removes her gloves, throwing them to the ground. He's horrified by what he sees. MOTHER comes running at the sound of VICTORIA's cries and picks up VICTORIA's gloves from the ground.*

MOTHER:     What have you done to her!

BROTHER:     I just wanted to see for myself!

*Then MOTHER sees VICTORIA's hands and is also horrified.*

MOTHER:     What have you done Victoria? What have you done to yourself?

*Both hands have a hole, a deep bloody hole through each palm, with strands of flesh and sinew falling from them as if both palms had been brutally gouged out. VICTORIA holds both palms up towards them and starts rising pushing her hands in their faces. MOTHER and BROTHER reel in terror.*

VICTORIA:     Why do you ask me? Why do you ask what you already know? I have not done this. This is not some pathetic attempt for your attention Mother, this not me trying to shock you brother. I am not the one who brought this upon myself. This is a gift; this is a gift from the Lord. I am blessed with the Lord's wounds, for I am His witness; I am

His bearer. Do you understand now? Do you believe now? *I* am here to save you brother. *I* am here to save all of you. This is my suffering; this is my price, for bearing your sins. Like my Lord, I shall bear your sins and you shall believe in me and believe in Him and repent. Repent brother. Repent from your life of sin, cast Satan and his minions away, come back to your one true Father, come back to your Lord.

## A CLAP OF THUNDER

*At the sound, VICTORIA lies prostrate as if stretched out on an upright plank of wood. The waiters still preparing the food in the kitchen come and hold VICTORIA aslant, with arms outstretched to each side. VICTORIA is paralyzed.*

VICTORIA:     This is it. It's happening. It's time for me to suffer the ultimate price. I can't stop it, pain is the one true path.

*Her MOTHER holds open her right palm and her BROTHER acts like he's hammering in the first nail. VICTORIA screams with each blow of the hammer. MOTHER & BROTHER go from the right palm to the left palm and finally the feet. Each nail takes seven blows of the hammer and, with each blow, VICTORIA screams in agonizing pain. Once done, VICTORIA is lifted, crucified,*

VICTORIA:     Oh lord, why have you abandoned
    me?

BLACKOUT

18

ONSCREEN – THE TALK

JOURNALIST & PSYCHOLOGIST

JOURNALIST:          Doctor, you have for many
    years promoted a theory based on the notion
    of mass hysteria to explain stigmatic and
    other religious supernatural phenomena; do
    you mean to say that these are all fakes?

PSYCH:          No, mass hysteria is not a hoax,
    nothing is faked. In a case of mass hysteria
    people do believe everything they see. Yet it
    is not always the case that what they believe
    they are witnessing corresponds directly
    with the physical reality of what is
    happening. And I am not saying these are all
    mad people either. The fact is that the brain
    is an extremely sensitive organ, even though
    we'd like to think that rationality and

emotions are completely separate functions of the brain, in fact, things are much more complicated than that and when you get the brain to function in extreme emotionally- and symbolically- charged scenarios, then one might never predict what the mind is going to show us or make manifest. This is why I believe that we may never have a purely objective and unbiased analysis in such extreme cases; this is also why, historically, we have always received reports of such phenomena through the presence of bystanders and witnesses believing that such reports are more believable. Yet those bystanders and those witnesses are part of the scenario that inform these very manifestations themselves. Such manifestations are there to be exhibited and the audience is part of the act.

JOURNALIST:		You mean that this is all a performance?

PSYCH:		A performance of the unconscious, where both actors and audience are unaware of their own desires and involvements in the act.

And the more people involved, the stronger the act becomes.

JOURNALIST: But what about doctors and other investigators? Are they also unconscious of what they are observing?

PSYCH: Nobody can ever be a hundred percent conscious of himself at any given moment, ever. There are always things going on inside your mind, thoughts, snippets of ideas, sensitive memories that may be shifting your behaviour one way or the other without you even noticing. We are very subtle animals and our perception is so easily influenced from both within and without. When a doctor is investigating a stigmatist, even though his medical profession is the main conscious reason for his being there, one may never know what he is bringing with him into that room. His past, his own faith and beliefs, his own preconceptions about such cases, his own needs and desires, everything, and everything is going to meet with what he finds in that room. When you have a religious mystic that has been bedridden for years in the same room having such extreme experiences for hours on end, something is bound to become entrenched in the room itself and I do not mean this in any supernatural manner. It could simply be a smell in the room, the colours in the room, symbols or idols the person chooses to place and have present in the room. We constantly wrap our most intimate environments around our own personalities and mental states. How can any observation made under such circumstances ever be in any manner purely objective?

JOURNALIST: So, you mean to say that any historical record or evidence of such cases can never be trusted?

PSYCH: To a certain extent no, we cannot trust any records as fact or as we would trust records made under normal circumstances. These are not normal circumstances, so any record created within that scenario is also bound to be influenced by the extreme abnormality of the situation itself. The observation becomes an extension of the exhibition so both become entrenched into a singular experience and thus the observation becomes itself inadmissible.

JOURNALIST: But doesn't this discredit too many professionals, both theist and atheist, who claim that their observations are honest?

PSYCH: I am not saying that they are not honest. I am saying that one can never vouch that what he is seeing is not being influenced or affected by an unknown factor. If a doctor who is a devout Catholic observes such phenomena and says there are no scientific explanations for these phenomena, one may say that he cannot find such explanations because he is a Catholic doctor. Whether that doctor admits it or not, it is still a fact that his faith influences in some way or other his perceptions and emotions at that moment in time. Same goes for the atheist doctor. If an atheist doctor says he has found an explanation than one may simply say that explanation is what the atheist is capable of perceiving given his intellectual and emotional state and condition at that point in time. This is why we always have such divergent opinions by so many different sources whenever we are investigating such cases. And no matter how much we try, these will never be cases we can study in a laboratory because of their culturally complex nature.

JOURNALIST: But it cannot possibly be only a matter of belief and opinion, right?

PSYCH: Unfortunately, as things stand, when it comes to explaining the source of these things, at this stage in history, it still is a matter of opinion. An informed opinion, yes, but still, an opinion. What is not a matter of opinion, and what we may all definitely agree on are two very clear phenomena; the religious devotion exhibited by these people and the immense physical and psychological pain and suffering they endure. These two factors are definitely real for both the witnesses and the stigmatists themselves because everybody believes they are real. These people truly believe that they are suffering the Passion of the Christ and for the human brain that is as good as actually suffering it, but who are we to say that that suffering is actually caused by God in a direct manner?

JOURNALIST: From your perspective there is no room for Divine Intervention?

PSYCH: Divine Intervention is a concept applied to plug in the holes in the sequence of cause and effect. I do not believe that we are ever in need of such a concept to explain what we do not yet understand. If there is a gap in our understanding, I call it a gap; not God. And there are so many things we still need to discover and understand about the complexity of our brain and its psycho-social mechanisms and effects that, to rush towards Divine Intervention as a definite explanation is immature, not to say irresponsible.

CUT TO JOURNALIST & BLOGGER

JOURNALIST: In your recent article on your blog, you've suggested that the facts regarding Victoria Sultana's last day are all and I quote "mired in contradictions and ambiguities". What do you really mean by this?

BLOGGER: It is as I wrote, black and white, the timeline of events that the Buhagiar family have presented to the media and keep insisting on is not believable. There are people that have confirmed how Victoria's husband, George, was not in fact at the Ministry that day. There are people that have seen Victoria entering a building for a High Council meeting at a time when she was supposed to be at her family home. There are others who claim she was present at a party in the evening when we're being told she actually died earlier. These are all serious contradictions that show how this family is covering something up whilst spinning this story for political mileage.

JOURNALIST:        But who are these witnesses? Where is your evidence?

BLOGGER:    We are living in a country where nobody dares to cross these powerful families. As a journalist, you know as well as I do that that's an unfair question. Fact is, we're living in a society where the rule of law cannot be trusted anymore because a small group of families and businesses have taken over the whole running of the state. Fine, there's the democratic vote, we hold an election every five years, blah blah blah. But in reality all the population is doing is choosing which corrupt group of individuals is going to receive the next blank cheque. Nobody is going to put their necks out against whoever is in power. So yes, all I have is my own conviction and the words of people that are afraid of showing their faces and giving their names because they know they'll end up without a job or bankrupt or worse, simply for speaking out.

JOURNALIST: So how can you keep spreading these allegations if you do not have any legally binding evidence to do so? Isn't this just spreading nasty rumours instead of actual investigative journalism?

BLOGGER: I will not wait for permission from the law to share what I believe is the truth. Our moral obligation for the truth goes beyond whatever the law permits or declares just. Justice, truth, freedom—these are values and virtues we have to strive for in any possible circumstance and the day we do so only within the limits of the law is the day our society becomes a stagnant one, a culture that has given up its spirit and is ready to die. I will keep sharing my views about these events and if not via journalism, I will find a way of doing it via a more artistic channel.

JOURNALIST: Even at the expense of tarnishing Victoria Sultana's reputation?

BLOGGER: Never. I am not the one tarnishing Victoria's reputation. It is true that throughout her life we never saw eye to eye, and we had a long history of disagreements. I am a liberal feminist and I always fought for liberal rights—LGBTQ, pro-choice rights etc. Of course, all that stands in direct opposition to what Victoria stood for. Within the printed milieu she considered me as her archnemesis and I thought of her as mine. Yet, today, if she were alive right now, if she had survived the events of that day, I believe that both of us would find it much easier to come to an agreement.

JOURNALIST: And what is that? What would Victoria Sultana agree with you on?

BLOGGER:     Both of us would agree on who the evil are. I sincerely believe that as I won't have any trouble putting aside my distaste for her religious beliefs, she would have no doubts about putting aside her principled opinions on the liberal rights movement, even if only for a few minutes, so both of us could agree on what's the true source of corruption plaguing our island; the greedy and power-hungry political class. The political elite are the true face of hypocrisy and evil, as they lie to and manipulate so many, stopping at nothing to get whatever they want for themselves, their families and their friends, at the expense of everybody else. So, our priority should always be to expose these people, make them drop their masks, left, right, whoever they are, and bring our readers, our audiences, the people, face to face with true evil. Hopefully, they might someday understand how those they idolize are nothing but wolves.

FADE TO BLACK

## 19

ONSTAGE

*Back onstage, the set is ready to receive the party. The caterers have created a buffet and bar area and some more festive lighting is put on. At this point, some members of the audience are invited to leave their seats and come for the party where they are given actual drinks and food. Some music is playing and MOTHER & BROTHER are mingling with the audience. All the characters from previous scenes are also present for the party. The audience is encouraged to chat and enjoy the party. UPSTAIRS is in the dark; the bedroom light is switched off though we can see that there is somebody asleep under the sheets. Nobody is allowed to go upstairs. After a few minutes, the music is lowered and BROTHER walks mid- way up the stairs to address the audience at the party.*

BROTHER:     You all undoubtedly know that my family, our entire legacy, has always been loyal to this political Party, loyal to its leadership and loyal to its vision for this country. Yet loyalty does not always mean conformity, and it is sometimes important to make sure that we are not mistaking apathy for obedience. Change is at hand. This is the time when all of us have to take stock of where we are and what we are doing, and for the sake of the future of this country, if necessary, change direction. Without change one does not prosper, and this is true for a whole country as much as it is for an individual. Thus, I'm taking the first step by resigning from my post as a member of the European Parliament to have more time for my country where it needs me most, here and in our own Parliament. You are all my trusted partners in my political career, I know that you have always supported me in my initiatives, so I have invited you here this evening to ask once again for your support, loyalty and faith. Thank you all for coming and enjoy the party.

*At a point towards the second half of the speech, VICTORIA slowly rises in bed upstairs. She reaches for the lamp and switches it on. She looks at her palms to find them bandaged but with thick stains of blood. Her BROTHER continues with the speech, even if what VICTORIA does upstairs starts getting the attention of the audience. She rises out of bed to find herself in her underwear. She has bandages around both her palms and her feet and a large bandage on her abdomen. Thick blood stains are visible at the positions of her wounds. Blood is also falling from her scalp onto her face. She is extremely thin, and what flesh we see is emaciated. Slowly, she exits her room and starts descending the stairs behind her BROTHER. VICTORIA descends slowly with arms*

*outstretched, exhibiting her wounds to everybody. She does
not react to her BROTHER or MOTHER or to what the
audience might do, she simply keeps descending in a slow but
steady pace as she chants Anima Christi.*

VICTORIA:    Anima Christi, sanctifica me

Corpus Christi, salva me

Sanguis Christi, inebria me

Aqua lateris Christi lava me

Passio Christi conforta me.

BROTHER:    What are you doing here?! Get back
up to bed! Have you truly gone mad?

*BROTHER tries to stop her from descending, terrified that
the audience will see her, but when she doesn't stop, he runs
to his MOTHER begging her to do something. MOTHER
simply kneels and starts praying with both hands held tightly
together, terrified to look VICTORIA in the face. The rest of
the crowd one by one falls to the floor, kneeling in horror and
prayer like MOTHER. Then BROTHER starts turning to
the audience for help.*

VICTORIA:    O bone Jesu, exaudi me, Intra Tua
vulnera, absconde me,

Ne permittas me separari a te. Ab
hoste maligno defende me.

> In hora mortis meae voca me. Et
> iube me venire ad te,
>
> Ut cum Sanctis tuis laudem te. In
> saecula saeculorum.

*VICTORIA stops centre stage with her MOTHER praying at her feet. VICTORIA falls in her MOTHER's arms, and from her MOTHER's arms she howls one final line.*

VICTORIA:   Forgive them Father. Forgive them, for they know not what they do.

*VICTORIA dies.*

*BROTHER howls in anger and disgust as the audience looks on aghast. He goes to one of the buffet tables and overturns it. MOTHER remains sobbing with VICTORIA in her arms.*

MOTHER:   This is our fault; we deserve hell. What have we done?

BROTHER:   No! This won't stop me; this won't change anything. (*Turning to the audience on stage in a terrifying rage*) Listen all of you, all of you here drinking my wine and eating my food, listen carefully. If any of you ever dare speak of what transpired here tonight, there will be hell to pay! What happened here, stays here, forever! NOT A SINGLE WORD! Or I will ruin you! RUIN YOU!

EXIT BROTHER

20

ENTER HUSBAND

*HUSBAND enters and approaches the scene in disbelief. He takes the dead VICTORIA from MOTHER's arms and places her on the floor.*

MOTHER:    What have we done?

HUSBAND:    We killed her. We killed her.

MOTHER:    Oh my God. With all our lies and plans and…but how could we have known?

HUSBAND:    We knew and we were merciless. We believed God would show her mercy, so we showed her none.

*In the meantime, the waiters bring a white bed sheet and spread it out on the floor.*

MOTHER:    We can't leave her like this.

*HUSBAND & MOTHER ask the audience to help them. They lift VICTORIA and lay her on the bed sheet. HUSBAND takes VICTORIA's gloves from MOTHER's*

*hands, kisses them, and places them on VICTORIA's chest,
then they wrap her in the bed sheet covering her up to her face.
She's placed centre stage and HUSBAND & MOTHER
kneel at her sides, with the audience surrounding them. They
ask the audience to pray with them. The EPILOGUES appear
on screen.*

EVERYONE:   Our Father who art in heaven,
hallowed be thy name. Thy kingdom come.
Thy will be done, on Earth as it is in
heaven…

*The lights fade to black before the prayer is finished.*

BLACKOUT

# Epilogues

ONSCREEN

Elizabeth, Victoria's mother, refused to answer any questions. She hasn't been seen outside her home since the event of her daughter's death.

······

Pierre, Victoria's brother, has become Party leader but his Party hasn't won a single general election since.

······

George, Victoria's husband, was found dead in the back garden of their home two days after he recorded the interviews. He died by hanging.

······

"If any man's work shall be burned, he shall suffer loss: but he himself shall be saved; yet so as by fire."
1 Corinthians 3:15

## The End